DARING
ESCAPES

DARING ESCAPES

by Anthony Masters
Illustrated by Ian Heard

W
FRANKLIN WATTS
LONDON•SYDNEY

Editor-in-Chief John C. Miles
Designer Jason Billin/Billin Design Solutions
Art Director Jonathan Hair

Cover artwork by Mark Bergin

First published in 2000
by Franklin Watts
96 Leonard Street
London
EC2A 4XD

Franklin Watts Australia
56 O'Riordan Street
Alexandria
NSW 2015

ISBN 0 7496 3725 0 (hbk)
        0 7496 4008 1 (pbk)

Dewey classification: 904

A CIP catalogue record for this book is available
from the British Library.

Printed in Great Britain

CONTENTS

GETTING OFF
THE MOUNTAIN

■ CHAPTER ONE

The shelling was terrifying. It went on all night, blasting the Argentinians on Mount Longdon. Bits of soldiers were everywhere.

Luis had never wanted to go to war. It was 1982 and the Argentinian and British armies were fighting fiercely in the Battle of the Falklands.

Luis had been forced to join the army. He had been hastily trained in Argentina. Now he was in a bunker on bleak Mount Longdon in the Falklands. At first he managed to put up with the freezing cold, spending his guard duty gazing up at the stars.

At night the sky cleared after days of fog and rain. The stars were the same as the ones he would have seen when he was at home in Argentina. He found that comforting.

But soon artillery bombardments increased. During the day, land gunners started firing on the Argentinian positions on Mount Longdon. During the evening and on into the night the British Navy would join in.

The constant shelling made Luis desperate to get away. One day he decided he had to escape from the mountain whatever the risk.

That night Luis's guard duty was made even worse because he could hear strange voices. They seemed to come and go on the wind. Now Luis was wondering if it was just his imagination.

Then one of his comrades began to hear the voices too.

'Password!' yelled a sentry. He was certain he had seen a soldier approaching. 'You've got to give the password.'

Shots cracked out and bullets flew across the slopes of the mountain.

CHAPTER TWO

No one was hit. But the sentries thought they had been surrounded by British soldiers. Or were they just passing by? The bunker overlooked a path that ran up the north-west side of the mountain.

There was no attack.

The next night, Luis heard the voices again, and suddenly he heard screaming. It seemed to be coming from a small valley in the mountains just behind them.

Then all hell broke loose.

Grenades exploded, machine guns clattered and rifle fire blazed away.

Luis crawled out of his bunker and lay flat. He was clutching his rifle. It hadn't been fired since he was on the training range in Argentina and that had been a year ago.

He could see shadows coming up the mountain path towards him. Trembling with fear, he lay still as the British soldiers leapt from rock to rock.

Nearby, a soldier fired. But he hadn't seen Luis yet.

Luis knew he had to do his duty. But he had never shot to kill before. He took aim and fired two or three times.

The soldier stopped shooting and there was a long, terrifying silence. Luis couldn't work out whether he had killed or just wounded him. Or was the soldier completely unhurt and even now crawling towards him?

Luis's partner Roberto came out of the bunker to join him. More shadows were moving through the rocks towards them now. Roberto tried to fire his machine gun, but only one round went off instead of a burst. Roberto tried again but the same thing happened.

They were both in a dangerously exposed position and they had to move. But where? He could hear the screams of the wounded and the groans of the dying. The terrible sounds echoed in Luis's head all day and all night. Maybe they would stay in his head for the rest of his life.

Luis knew the main battle was raging in the valley and it would be crazy to go down there. So they both crawled backwards on their hands and knees. Eventually Luis and Roberto reached another position in the rocks with a small path below them.

Although they could have kept out of sight, Luis and Roberto began firing on the British soldiers as they came up the path. This time, the British saw the two Argentinian soldiers and began to fire back at them. The bullets thudded around the rocks. Luis knew he could be hit at any moment.

■ CHAPTER THREE

Suddenly the British stopped firing and there was another horrible silence.

Were they hoping Luis and Roberto would show themselves? Still nothing happened. Except for the distant sounds of battle, the night was still.

They waited. And waited.

Suddenly Luis and Roberto couldn't bear the tension any longer. They started firing again.

The British fired back immediately. This time they went on shooting for so long that Luis was numbed by the constant noise.

Then there was the terrifying silence again.

This time, they lay on the damp ground in the raw cold of the night. Roberto and Luis were too afraid to start firing again. They stayed there in silence for over half an hour.

The fighting in the valley seemed to have died down, but they didn't know who had won.

There were still a few rifle shots and some shouting.

Luis knew they had to make a decision. Their command area was in the valley. Now everything was so much quieter, they should try and get back to it.

Sweating despite the cold, they crawled through the rocks – and listened. Then they began to crawl again, and froze. They could hear English voices.

Luis looked over the top of a rock and saw a couple of British soldiers. He began to wonder if the British had won the battle and were taking prisoners.

He could have shot both of them, but the noise would only bring more British soldiers.

Luis knew he and Roberto had to keep out of sight. He was afraid of being taken prisoner at night. Anything could happen. The British might shoot them instead.

They crawled back into the rocks
to try and find a better hiding place.
Just as they had found somewhere,
more British soldiers appeared.

They moved closer and closer to
them.

One of the soldiers was talking into his radio.

Did the soldiers know where Luis and Roberto were? Could they just be playing a game?

CHAPTER FOUR

Luis sweated and prayed and sweated some more. So did Roberto. They both knew that any movement on their part could bring instant death.

Then the British soldiers moved on. Luis and Roberto shook with relief.

Somehow they survived the night, curled up in the rocks, certain that they were surrounded by the British.

Luis couldn't decide which was worse – hiding on the freezing cold mountain or being shot by the British. But suppose they were allowed to surrender peacefully? That would be his only way of escaping safely from

Mount Longdon. But if they decided not to take prisoners and he was shot – then he would be escaping life itself.

At dawn, they could both see a British soldier standing nearby with his back to them.

Luis nodded at Roberto and they both stood up. They didn't really know what they were going to do. But the soldier seemed to have eyes in the back of his head. He swung round and shot at them with his rifle.

Luis flung himself on the ground.

Roberto froze, unable to move.

The shots missed.

Luis lay there, waiting for the soldier to fire again. He was sure the bullets would soon tear into him.

But nothing happened.

When he dared to look up again, he saw Roberto was waving a piece of paper. He was going to surrender for both of them.

◼ CHAPTER FIVE

Would the British soldier understand?
Would he let them surrender?

The soldier beckoned them over. But
he was still pointing his rifle at them.

Luis and Roberto walked slowly
towards him with their hands raised
above their heads. In the grey light of
dawn they could see dead bodies lying
around the slopes.

But they were too afraid to look
closely. Even now Luis knew they
could be shot at any moment.

As soon as Luis reached the
soldier, more British troops arrived
and pushed him to the ground. They

made him lie there, face down. Then his jacket was stripped off and his bootlaces removed.

When they had checked him for weapons, they told him to stay where he was. Roberto had to do the same.

In the early morning light Luis could now see a line of other Argentinian prisoners. The British soldiers pushed Luis and Roberto into the line. Were they all going to be marched to the firing squad? Or was there still a chance they would be sent to a prisoner-of-war compound? Luis couldn't tell.

All he did know was that this might not be the kind of escape from Mount Longdon he had hoped for.

■ CHAPTER SIX

The column was marched off in single
file. Luis was sure that the British
soldiers were looking for a place to
shoot them all. As soon as a spot was
found they would face the firing squad.

Luis thought of his family back in
Argentina and felt like crying.

If only he and Roberto hadn't given
themselves up they might still be lying

hidden among the cold rocks of the mountain.

The prisoners were marched down the western slope. Then the British told them to sit down in a group.

By early evening, helicopters were flying to and fro, moving prisoners. Still Luis, Roberto and their companions were left where they were.

Then the group was moved on about two kilometres. This time they were told to sit in a circle. The night was cold and they sat close together to keep warm. Most of the prisoners were praying.

Next morning, more helicopters arrived and the Argentinian soldiers were flown to the town of Fitzroy in the East Falklands. When the prisoners arrived, they were given food, drink and medical help. The prisoners were then taken out of the town to a big sheep farm and placed in sheep pens.

Luis had never felt so happy. No one was going to be shot after all. He was being fed and looked after. When the war was over maybe he would be able to go home.

Above all, he had escaped from the bleak horrors of Mount Longdon – horrors that would remain in his mind for the rest of his life.

Luis had never wanted to go to war.

ESCAPE THROUGH OCCUPIED FRANCE

■ CHAPTER ONE

They rested by day and marched in a single line by night. Tonight Lieutenant Broad was in front, the sergeant at the rear. When dawn came, the Seaforths hid at the edge of a wood and slept for a while.

The date was June 1940. The place was German-occupied France. The French had just surrendered to the Germans and the British soldiers were trapped on the Havre Peninsula.

Lieutenant Richard Broad of the Seaforth Highlanders was in charge of seven Scotsmen. None of them could speak French.

Broad was faced with the choice of staying with the wounded to surrender, or making what seemed an impossible journey back to England. He decided on the journey.

Broad had to make up his mind which way to go. He told his men: 'If the port of Le Havre is still in the hands of the Allies we might be able to find a boat to get us back to England. If the Germans have taken the port, we'll be caught. But it's a risk we're going to have to take.'

Now in their hiding place in the wood the little group slept. But three hours later they were woken by the sound of revving engines and men's voices.

Broad realised they had accidentally camped alongside an enemy unit.

He turned to his men and whispered, 'Creep away one at a time.'

They spent the rest of the day hidden in the long grass of a field of hay.

German transport horses watched the soldiers for some time and then lost interest. When their drivers arrived to feed them, they passed within metres of the British hiding places. Then a Frenchman, the owner of the field, walked past with his wife.

There could be no doubt that the farmer had seen them. For a moment, Broad was sure he was going to give them away.

But the farmer told his wife to be careful. 'Don't tread on the Englishmen,' he said.

As they slowly walked away Broad sighed with relief. But how could they avoid the Germans? They seemed to be everywhere. Surely they would soon be arrested.

Broad told himself to think more positively. So far they were free – and he was determined the Seaforths would stay that way.

CHAPTER TWO

As the day drew on, Broad wondered if it had been a bad mistake to travel inland. Maybe they should have tried to escape via the coast where there might be fewer Germans. But he had to keep going or the men would lose faith in him.

When darkness fell they were able to move on. But after the Seaforths had been marching for an hour, they were seen by a German soldier who fired his gun at them.

The British were crossing an open field at the time and luckily the shots alarmed a herd of cows.

Terrified, the cows ran about in all
directions and this gave the Seaforths
some cover. Broad and his men dived
under a barbed-wire fence and ran
for it. Strangely, none of the Germans
followed.

Broad was puzzled. Were they
being driven into some kind of trap?
Were they being played with by the

Germans in a cat and mouse game? He didn't fancy being a mouse.

Later, he saw a searchlight beam criss-crossing the sky and he realised the soldiers were part of a searchlight detachment. They were looking out for low-flying Allied planes.

Suddenly more searchlights from other detachments joined in. The whole landscape was lit up in a harsh glare.

The Seaforths froze, not daring to move. At any moment they could be picked out by one of the beams. Then they heard the sound of a plane, flying low, flashing signals. Did the Germans think it was one of their own?

The plane wasn't fired on.

Then Broad and his men heard a
different note in the engines. Was the
plane in trouble? The searchlight
crews didn't seem to notice and
switched off their beams.

The Seaforths were plunged back
into darkness.

The plane was now making a low
roaring sound.

Suddenly it seemed to be coming straight at them.

'Get down,' whispered Broad. 'Get down now!'

They threw themselves to the ground.

A hot blast flattened the grass and there was a grinding crash.

Flames leapt to the sky about a hundred metres away.

Once again, the Seaforths ran through the night.

■ CHAPTER THREE

The following morning, the Seaforth Highlanders reached a field of corn and hid there for the day. They had no water or food. Broad meant them to stay there until it became dark.

But hunger got the better of them.

'We'll be too weak to move if we don't eat something,' Broad told the Seaforths.

Broad and Turner set out to see what they could find.

As they approached a farmhouse, a large open jeep came down the drive.

Broad and Turner dived into a field of spring greens, for they had seen

German uniforms.

The two men lay with their faces pressed to the earth. To their dismay they realised the field had only just been covered with manure.

The jeep skidded to a halt outside the farmhouse. Broad reckoned the Germans must be about 75 metres away. He heard a door slam.

Could they have been seen?

Broad still had a gun. If he heard footsteps he would fire. A voice rang out in German and there was a soft reply.

A long silence followed. Then the door slammed again and the jeep started up, engine revving and tyres screaming on the gravel.

There was silence again.

Stuffing the spring greens into their battledress, Broad and Turner hurried back to their comrades.

The greens were full of grit and

manure and made a bad meal. As a result, the Seaforths were even more thirsty.

■ CHAPTER FOUR

The march across the French
countryside that night was very hard.

The Seaforths were all hungry and
thirsty. They were beginning to feel
very ill indeed.

Then they came across two tied-up
cows. But their desperate attempts
to milk them failed miserably. Broad
looked at his men in despair and saw
one of them was missing. Where had
Dodd got to?

They went back the way they had
come and found him at last, asleep
under a tree. Broad grabbed his
shoulders and yelled in his ear.

'Wake up,' he said. 'You can't go to sleep here!'

Dodd had to be dragged to his feet to get him moving again.

The Seaforths then followed a

railway line until it arrived at a level crossing. There was also an empty keeper's cottage. In the garden, to their joy, the Seaforths found a well full of water.

Too much drink can be dangerous if you haven't had any for days. But the Seaforths drank a lot. At long last they didn't feel thirsty any more.

Then they began to look around for food. But there was nothing. The next day, however, they found a jar of salted butter in an empty house. Later they discovered a field of potatoes. They were only small, but coated with the salted butter the potatoes made the most wonderful meal in the world.

Twenty-four hours later, Broad decided they couldn't live on scraps of food found here and there. They had to have a better diet or they would be too weak to walk. But this would mean going to a village. The people who lived there might give them away.

Broad decided they had to take a big risk.

From the shelter of a wood, he noticed a woman milking a cow. His chance had come and he had to act on it.

Covered by Turner who was always with him on his morning patrol, Broad climbed down a bank. He was watched by two small boys.

'Excuse me,' said Broad. 'We're desperate for food and water. Can you help us?'

The woman went on milking the cow.

Broad continued to ask for food and water.

After a while the woman agreed to

bring eggs and milk to the wood where the rest of the Seaforths were hidden.

Broad had only just thanked her when he heard the sound of a car. He ran up the bank and hid behind it with Turner.

Broad drew out his revolver and peered over the bank. The car, loaded with German officers, came to a halt beside the hedge. One of the officers asked the way. The woman told him.

Still the two small boys watched.

Broad waited for the woman to give them away. He also waited for the boys to do the same. He had his finger on the trigger of his gun.

But no one gave them away.

One of the Germans thanked the woman for her help. Then they turned the car round and drove off.

That night the Seaforths had their first proper meal of hard-boiled eggs and milk. The woman wouldn't take any money from them.

Broad was pleased by the woman's kindness. The French were clearly willing to help the British army. If they did, the British might be able to free them from the Germans.

When the Seaforths reached a town, they found the local people just as helpful. Without their kindness the British could not have survived.

Later, they reached the River Seine and managed to cross it on a home-made raft.

But the escape back to England took much longer than Broad could ever have imagined. After a year of hiding out in the houses of the French, cycling and sleeping rough, the Seaforth Highlanders finally reached Gibraltar.

They had managed to escape through France and into Spain. At last they arrived in London. They had marched a very long way round, but under Broad's daring leadership the Seaforths had made it.

THE DIRT ROAD

■ CHAPTER ONE

Peter Maas was sure that the longer he stayed in Bosnia, the more likely he was to die there.

Maas was an American newspaper journalist. In 1992 he was in Bosnia, writing reports for *The Washington Post.*

On a scorching summer's day, Peter, Jonathan (another reporter), and Vlatka (an interpreter), set out to search for a prison camp where Bosnian Muslims were being held – probably in very poor conditions.

Peter and Jonathan had heard rumours that the Serbs had

decided to start prison camps and
they wanted to find one. The story
would make front-page news.

'Trying to find this camp is going
to be really dangerous,' Peter warned
Jonathan. 'The Serbs may kill us to
stop our reports appearing in the
newspapers.'

But in Bosnia Jonathan and Peter risked being killed every day.

Peter was picked up from his hotel in Belgrade at 9.00 am by Jonathan and Vlatka.

The journalists and their interpreter drove out of Belgrade in a BMW and crossed over a railway bridge into the Serb-controlled part of Bosnia.

After a while, they turned off the main road and headed down a country lane.

There were cornfields on either side and the sun blazed down.

'There's a road block,' said Jonathan, stamping on the brakes of the BMW.

But it wasn't the usual kind of road

block with soldiers in uniform armed with Kalashnikov rifles. Soldiers acted under orders from a commander.

This one was different. It only had four men with hunting rifles.

Peter felt a chill of fear. Many of the men from the villages were primitive and fierce. They still felt angry at being defeated in battle by the Turks in the fourteenth century. They would think nothing of shooting to kill.

'What are you doing here?' demanded their leader, who was wearing a tatty-looking uniform from World War II. He was in his early sixties.

'We're here to visit the prison camp,' said Vlatka.

'There is no prison camp. Get out,' the older man replied angrily.

'So why is there a road block if there's no prison camp?' asked Peter.

The old man explained there was fighting ahead and they would be in danger if they drove on any further.

Then the guards aimed their hunting rifles at them and Peter suddenly realised they were drunk.

CHAPTER TWO

Peter had learnt that in Bosnia it was never wise to argue with an armed man. Journalists who didn't remember that rule were usually killed.

They drove a mile back down the road and stopped again. It had taken them two hours to reach this place and neither Peter nor Jonathan wanted to leave without a story.

'Let's talk to the locals,' suggested Jonathan.

There were a few non-Serbian people living in the area who might tell them something.

The journalists stopped at a house

that belonged to gypsies.

'Are you here to see the prison camp?' the gypsy woman asked.

She went on to tell them that buses full of prisoners with shaven heads were driven through the village to the prison camp every week.

She pointed to a dirt road that went through the cornfields and by-passed the road block.

Peter checked again at another gypsy house and was told the same story. As they were talking he saw a man slowly leave the house on his bicycle.

Sitting in the BMW, Peter, Jonathan and Vlatka tried to work out the risks they were taking. But they already

knew it was very dangerous. There
could be another road block with
more drunken, trigger-happy thugs.

Worse still, the four men at the
first road block might find out they
were still here asking questions. They
might return to shoot them.

'We could end up in an unmarked grave in one of those fields,' Peter warned the others.

'Why don't we go back to our hotel in Belgrade?' he suggested. 'We could all go up to my room. It would be good to have a drink and a talk.'

The dirt road was hazed in dusty sunlight and didn't look inviting. In fact the road looked very threatening.

The journalists looked at each other.

The search could end in death and disaster. All for a newspaper story.

Jonathan turned the car round.

They headed down the dirt road, like hounds on the scent of a fox.

CHAPTER THREE

Jonathan had only driven a few hundred metres down the dirt road when Peter asked, 'Why did that gypsy man cycle off on his bike while we were talking to his wife? Do you think he's an informer?'

'He could have cycled off to the road block,' said Jonathan. 'He might even be telling the drunken guards that a car full of journalists was heading for the prison camp.'

Peter felt cold with fear.

Jonathan was the first to notice the dust cloud on the road.

Soon a Yugo car drew up behind

them. Peter turned to see the men from the road block in the car. Their hunting rifles were sticking out of the windows. The driver was flashing the headlights and honking the horn.

They clearly wanted the journalists to stop.

'We've got to obey them,' said Peter.

In some ways, the thugs looked like characters from a comedy film. But he knew they were also dangerous.

Peter glanced at Jonathan and Vlatka. They were all wondering if there was any chance of escape. Peter now knew they had made a bad mistake. If he could have re-lived the last few hours he would have turned round at the first road block.

He felt a sick feeling in his stomach. If only they hadn't been so stupid as to take the dirt road.

But it was too late now.

Peter began to sweat and it had

nothing to do with the heat. When he glanced round at the others, he could see they were terrified too.

CHAPTER FOUR

Jonathan brought the BMW to a halt as the road block gang jumped out of their Yugo and ran towards them.

They were pointing their rifles at them and screaming.

The veins stood out in their foreheads as they furiously shouted abuse. Then Peter and Jonathan had to hand over their passports and United Nations press passes.

The thugs took the documents. They told the journalists to follow them in their car. Then they got back into the Yugo.

To Peter's horror, the Yugo drove

deep into one of the cornfields.

No one spoke in the BMW.

This was what they had all feared.

They were going to be killed.

Jonathan wondered
if he could change gear
and back out of the cornfield.
But he knew there was no way he
could do this and drive away fast
enough.

'eter wanted to close his eyes and
. He felt like a scared child. He
ldenly knew how a Bosnian Muslim
ıst feel.

The Yugo began to slow down in
ıe middle of the corn.

Was this where they were all going
to die?

CHAPTER FIVE

Suddenly the Yugo made a U-turn. Jonathan and Peter gazed at the spurts of dust in amazement.

'They're heading back to the main road,' said Jonathan. 'Maybe we've got a chance.'

'They're more likely to be taking us to their commander. They may have to ask him if they can kill us,' Peter replied.

The Serbs led them back to the main road and Jonathan pulled up behind the Yugo outside a run-down café. One of the thugs went inside to make a call.

Vlatka noticed a middle-aged Muslim sipping a cup of coffee in the shade.

Peter guessed this Muslim must be loyal to the Serbs. Otherwise, he would have been in the prison camp down the road with a shaved head.

'Ramiz!' yelled the leader of the thugs. 'I told you never

to come here!'

He grabbed a bottle and slammed it against Ramiz's shoulders. Blood and glass flew everywhere.

Peter, Jonathan and Vlatka had to watch Ramiz being savagely beaten up.

They knew they couldn't do anything about it. If they did they would be shot.

CHAPTER SIX

Peter felt deeply ashamed. They had stood and watched a man being badly beaten. He now knew why the Serbs did nothing to help their Muslim neighbours when they were taken to the camps. They kept quiet because they were afraid for their own lives.

Peter knew this dreadful guilt would never leave him.

They were taken next to the military headquarters in the nearest town. But the commander didn't arrest them. Instead, he drove them to his own house where he gave them coffee and soft drinks.

Later the commander showed Peter, Jonathan and Vlatka videos of crimes committed against Serbs by Muslims and Croats over the years.

He denied the prison camp existed.

Then the commander let them go.

But neither Jonathan nor Peter were cowards.

Instead of returning to the safety of their hotel, they went into a barber's shop.

'My friends would like to talk to you and your customer,' said Vlatka.

Luckily both men were Muslims.

'They are American journalists,' explained Vlatka.

The barber put down his scissors. He locked the door and pulled the blinds down over the windows.

'What can you tell us about the prison camps?' asked Vlatka.

'Everything,' he whispered.

Peter and Jonathan began to take notes.

When they got back to their hotel, they had never felt so relieved in their lives.

Both men had taken a daring risk and had come back with an important story which would hit the headlines the next day.

GLOSSARY

Allies the British, Commonwealth, French, Russian and American nations who fought together against the Germans in World War II (1939-1945).

Argentina a South American country.

artillery heavy weapons of war, for example mounted guns, cannon and missile launchers.

bombardment an attack with heavy guns.

Bosnia one of countries of the former Yugoslavia.

bunker an underground bomb-proof shelter.

detachment a group of soldiers.

enemy unit a group of soldiers from the opposing army.

Falklands a group of islands in the South Atlantic Ocean belonging to the United Kingdom but claimed by Argentina.
The United Kingdom and Argentina fought a war over them in 1982.

Gibraltar small state situated in southern Spain, which belongs to the United Kingdom.

grenade a small bomb, thrown by hand.

Gypsies a race of people who used to wander through Europe in caravans but now often live in houses.

informer a person who gives information.

interpreter a person who explains what is being said.

jeep a light, four-wheel-drive military vehicle.

journalist someone who writes for a newspaper.

Kalashnikov rifle a gun manufactured by the Russians.

machine gun a quick-firing gun.

Muslim a person who follows the religion of Islam. In Bosnia the Muslims are a group of people who are persecuted by the Serbs.

persecution where one group of people attacks another group because they belong to a different race or hold religious beliefs different to their own.

press pass a document that shows you are a journalist and are allowed to travel freely.

prison camp a camp where prisoners-of-war and others are detained, often in horrible conditions.

revolver a hand gun.

road block a guarded checkpoint.

searchlight a light with a very powerful beam, used for picking out objects at night.

shelling shots fired from heavy guns.

trigger a lever that fires a gun.

Turks a people who live in Turkey. They ruled the former Yugoslavia for many years.

United Nations an association of states, set up after World War II to maintain world peace.

unmarked grave a grave without a tombstone.

Also available in this series

Football Heroes

*Cantona always looked very cool. He wore his
shirt collar casually turned up and his face showed
no interest in what was going on around him. That,
of course, was misleading; in fact, he was totally focused.*

*Read Football Heroes and find out about the thrilling
careers of some of the giants of football.*

Mountain Horror

Jon had to get himself going. He had to make decisions. Above all he needed a plan. If he slipped off the icy slope he would die at once. But that would be better than dying slowly on the mountain.

Read Mountain Horror and find out how climbers survived against all the odds.

Terror at Sea

Jacques and Frédéric thought they might be able to escape – that is, unless one of them got wounded. At the first sign of blood the sharks would attack them both.

Read Terror at Sea and find out about narrow escapes from a watery grave.